Invisible Strings

The Unsettling Power of Social Conformity and Group Manipulation

Freudian Trips

Disclaimer

The views and opinions expressed in this book are those of the author(s) and do not necessarily reflect the official policy or position of any other agency, organization, employer, or company. The contents of this book are for informational and educational purposes only and are not intended to serve as professional advice, diagnosis, or treatment.

The information provided in this book is believed to be accurate and reliable as of the date of publication. However, it may include some errors or inaccuracies, and no warranty or guarantee is provided regarding the accuracy, timeliness, or applicability of the content.

Readers are encouraged to consult with professional philosophers, educators, or other qualified professionals where appropriate for personalized advice. The author(s) and publisher shall not be liable for any loss, damage, or harm caused or alleged to be caused, directly or indirectly, by the information or ideas contained, suggested, or referenced in this book.

By reading this book, the reader acknowledges and agrees that they are solely responsible for how they interpret and apply the information contained herein.

This book may also include references to other works, studies, and sources. These references are provided for further reading and exploration and do not imply endorsement or validation of the specific theories, viewpoints, or interpretations presented in those works.

Chapter 1: Introduction

Invisible Strings: An Unfiltered Peek into Why We Act the Way We Do

Have you ever found yourself nodding along in a group, even if you disagreed? Or wearing that new fashion trend just because everyone else was? If you've ever wondered why we sometimes go with the flow or what power groups have over our decisions, you're about to embark on a fascinating journey.

Understanding Social Psychology

Imagine you're sitting in a giant theater, and life is the movie playing. Social psychology is like those special glasses that allow you to see the hidden layers behind the scenes. It's all about understanding how we think, feel, and act when we're around other people. Think of it as the science of "us in groups."

If life was a game, social psychology helps us understand the rules. Rules not written in any book but in the invisible dance of human interactions. When we laugh, when we follow, when we rebel—it's all part of this vast, intricate dance.

The Scope and Relevance of Conformity and Group Influence

Now, imagine you're at a party. Music is loud, and people are dancing. Suddenly, everyone starts doing the same dance move. You don't know the move, but in a minute, you find your feet moving to the same rhythm. Why?

This is where the topics of conformity and group influence come in.

Conformity is a bit like peer pressure. It's the act of changing our behavior or thinking to fit in with others around us. It's not always a bad thing. After all, if we didn't conform at all, society would be a wild mix of confusion! But, sometimes, it means we're suppressing what we truly believe or feel.

Group influence goes a step beyond. It's the power a group has to shape our opinions, decisions, and even our view of what's right and wrong. If you've ever supported a sports team and felt the infectious energy of the crowd around you, you've felt group influence.

Overview of Book Structure and Purpose

In "Invisible Strings," we'll untangle the complex web of human interactions. We'll explore why we often act in ways just because others are doing it. We'll uncover stories of real people, just like you, who found themselves under the spell of the group, and what they did about it.

This journey will be divided into different sections:

Why do we conform? We'll dive into the science and the heart of why we sometimes suppress our own voices.

Real-life dramas. Stories of people who stood up against the tide or got swept away by it.

The digital age and group influence. How are platforms like social media changing the game?

Breaking free. Tips and strategies to hold onto your unique voice and stand your ground.

By the end, you'll have not just a better understanding of the world around you, but also the tools to navigate it with confidence.

Join me on this journey as we explore the unseen forces that shape our lives. It promises to be eye-opening, maybe even life-changing. But most importantly, it'll be a journey of self-discovery as you learn more about yourself and the invisible strings that might be pulling you.

Chapter 2: What's Pulling Our Strings? Understanding Conformity and Group Influence

Imagine you're in a big city, standing in the midst of a bustling crowd. Everyone starts looking up at the sky. Would you resist the urge to look up too? Well, that's a tiny taste of the forces we're about to delve into. Buckle up, and let's dive in!

What Exactly is Conformity?

Have you ever felt like doing something just because everyone else was doing it? That's conformity in action. In simple words, conformity is our natural tendency to act or think like the members of a group. It's like when you find yourself humming along to a popular song even if you didn't initially like it.

The Different Flavors of Conformity

Conformity isn't just one size fits all. It has different shades:

"I want to fit in!" - This is when we do something mainly to be accepted by others. Like wearing that quirky hat because everyone in school is wearing it. Even if, deep down, you don't quite like it.

"They probably know better!" - This is when we copy others because we believe they have more knowledge about a situation than we do. Imagine you're in a new city and everyone at a pedestrian crossing waits for a signal light you can't see. You'd probably wait too, assuming they know something you don't.

Group Influence: More than Just Peer Pressure

Now, while conformity is about us tweaking our behaviors to match others, group influence is the power that the group has over individual members. It's like a magnetic force that pulls our beliefs, feelings, and behaviors in a certain direction. Remember when you cheered for a team simply because everyone else was cheering for them? That's group influence at work!

Let's Talk 'Norms'

Have you noticed that in most elevators, people face the door? It's an unwritten rule. No one says it, but we all do it. This silent, mutual understanding is what we call a norm.

Norms are standards or guidelines shared by members of a group about how they should behave. They're like invisible hands guiding our actions—most of the time, we don't even realize they're there. But they play a huge role in shaping our behavior.

Getting into the Nuances: Normative and Informational Influence

Now, before we venture further, let's quickly touch on two big words that are actually simple concepts:

Normative Influence - This is the pressure we feel to fit in so that we're liked and accepted by others. It's that little voice inside saying, "Do it, or they might think you're weird!" Remember the quirky hat example? That was normative influence nudging you.

Informational Influence - This comes into play when we're unsure about something, so we look to others for guidance. It's like walking into a room and sitting down because everyone else is, even if you're not sure why. You trust that the group knows what's happening.

So, there we have it! The invisible forces that sometimes shape our decisions—conformity and group influence. Whether it's choosing a new hairstyle, picking a restaurant, or even the bigger decisions in life, these forces are often at play. But by understanding them, we can decide when we want to go with the flow or swim against the tide. After all, knowing is half the battle. The next chapters will delve deeper into these forces, so keep those special glasses on and stay tuned!

Chapter 3: The Inner Workings of Conformity

Conformity often feels like an invisible pull, subtly guiding our behavior. But where does its power come from? Let's peek behind the curtain at some of the main theories that explain why we fall under the spell of the group.

Social Comparison Theory

Humans are like lost sheep, constantly looking around to see what others are doing. That's the essence of social comparison theory. We compare our own behavior and opinions to those around us, using others as a guide for what is normal or right. No one wants to feel like an oddball, so we unconsciously adjust to match the herd. Makes you wonder - if everyone jumped off a bridge, would we all follow?

Normative Social Influence Theory

This one says we conform because we want to be accepted by the group. When norms are established, failing to follow those unwritten rules gets you dirty looks or rejection. So we conform to fit in, even if it means hiding parts of our true selves. The dizzying power of wanting to belong...

Informational Social Influence Theory

Sometimes we go with the flow simply because we trust the wisdom of the crowd. Assume a room full of art critics loves a painting - you'd probably play it safe and praise it too. This theory focuses on when we conform because we believe the group has more expertise than little old us. Safety in numbers, right? Or is it...

Social Identity Theory

This implies that the groups we are a part of define who we are as individuals. We conform to strengthen our connection to that group and the identity it provides. The lure of belonging is so strong that our individual voices fade into the background. But is blending in with the tribe worth vanishing into the crowd?

So which theory explains why we all start dancing the same moves? Perhaps a blend of wanting to fit in, seek wisdom in numbers, and feel part of something bigger than ourselves. The deep human desire to belong can lead us willingly into conformity's embrace. But the true dance comes when we learn to waltz to the beat of our own drums.

Chapter 4: Unmasking the Human Mind: Riveting Experiments and Their Revelations

Imagine you're part of a reality show where people's reactions to different scenarios are tested. Some of these scenes look straight out of a movie, but they reveal deep secrets about how we act around others. That's precisely what these iconic experiments did. Let's dive into some real-life 'episodes' of the most talked-about social psychology experiments and their jaw-dropping findings!

Solomon Asch's "Which Line is Longer?" Game

Imagine you're in a room with several people, and you're all asked a simple question: which of the three lines shown to you matches the length of a given line? Sounds easy, right?

But, here's the twist: almost everyone in the room, except you, starts picking the wrong line. On purpose. What would you do? Stick to what you know is right or just go along with the crowd?

Solomon Asch tested this scenario. And guess what? Many people chose the incorrect line, just because everyone else did! This experiment showcased how powerful the need to fit in can be, even when we're sure about the right answer.

Stanley Milgram's "Shocking" Lesson in Obedience

Now, this is a twisty one. Imagine you're told to give electric shocks to a person in another room every time they answer a question incorrectly. With each wrong answer, you have to increase the shock's intensity, even if you hear them scream in pain. Would you continue just because an authority figure told you to?

Stanley Milgram wanted to understand how far people would go in obeying orders. Astoundingly, many participants went on to deliver what they believed were lethal shocks, just because they were told to. This experiment gave a chilling glimpse into how far people might go when following orders, especially from authority figures.

Philip Zimbardo's Chilling Prison Roleplay

Imagine signing up for an experiment where you're randomly assigned to be a prison guard or a prisoner in a mock prison setup. Sounds like an innocent role-playing game, right?

Philip Zimbardo's Stanford Prison Experiment did just that. But things quickly turned dark. The "guards" began displaying authoritative and abusive behavior, while the "prisoners" showed signs of extreme stress and passivity. The study had to be stopped after just six days, even though it was intended to last two weeks.

This experiment revealed the frightening speed at which people could slip into roles, especially when power dynamics are at play.

New Age Discoveries: The Latest Scoop

While those classic experiments gave deep insights into human behavior, recent research has used technology and modern methodologies to shed more light. Studies now show the impact of digital life and social media on conformity and group influence. For instance, "liking" something on social media because others have liked it, or changing our opinions based on viral trends. The realm of online conformity is vast, ever-evolving, and a topic we'll dive into deeper in upcoming chapters.

In a nutshell, these experiments teach us that the human mind is a complex web, easily influenced by peers, authority, and roles we are thrown into. But by knowing and understanding these influences, we can be more aware, make conscious choices, and perhaps, rewrite our story. As we progress through this book, we'll explore more tools and techniques to recognize when these influences are at play and how to keep our true selves shining through.

Chapter 5: Tug of War: What Pulls us Toward Conformity

Conformity whispers in our ears like a subtle voice, gently urging us to follow the pack. But when does it speak loudly versus barely murmur? Let's explore key factors that turn up the volume on conformity's call.

Group Size

A lone voice of dissent can echo boldly in a smaller gathering. But as the crowd grows, individual voices fade into the chorus. Researchers found conformity shoots up in groups bigger than three, when standing alone feels untenable.

Unanimity and Dissent

Nothing ushers us into conformity like the unanimous agreement of others. But a lone rebel yelling "stop!" awakens our own independent streak. Conformity is a fragile thing, easily shaken by a courageous soul willing to dissent.

Cohesiveness and Group Membership

The more we feel part of the "in crowd", the tighter conformity's grip. If we barely know the group, their norms don't hold much sway. But when we desperately want to fit in and be accepted, oh how we conform.

Culture and Conformity

Culture whispers expectations into our minds from birth about how to act, think, speak. Some cultures value harmony over individualism, making conformity seem honorable. Others celebrate rugged individualism. Our culture charts our path.

Individual Characteristics

Confident, defiant types often dance to their own beat. Timid souls follow the song of the crowd. Our personality and values act like a shield against conformity...or leave us exposed to its influence.

In the end, conformity's strength depends on how firmly its strings are tied to human nature's longing to connect. When we feel isolated, conformity's call is a siren song. Connectedness is the heart's true desire.

Chapter 6: The Double-Edged Sword: When Going with the Flow Helps and Hurts

Imagine you're on a teeter-totter, trying to maintain balance. On one side, you have the pull to fit in, to go with the flow, and on the other, the push to stand out, to be unique. This delicate balance has consequences, some that light up our world, and others that cast shadows. Let's explore both sides.

The Yin and Yang of Conformity

Every coin has two sides, and so does conformity:

The Bright Side: Ever found yourself humming to a tune just because it's popular and everyone's listening to it? That shared love for a song brings people together. Conformity helps build social harmony. It's why traffic systems work — everyone agrees to follow the same set of rules, creating order.

The Dark Side: But what if everyone's humming a tune that promotes hate or division? Simply agreeing without questioning can lead to spreading harmful beliefs. Blindly following the crowd can sometimes stifle individuality and even lead to harmful actions.

Conformity: The Invisible Puppeteer of Society

When we all follow certain rules or norms, it's easier to predict behaviors and maintain order. This is called social control. It's like an invisible hand that guides how we behave. For instance, waiting in line is a form of social control; we do it because it's the accepted norm and it ensures fairness. But, when this control becomes too restrictive, it can limit creativity and freedom.

When Groups Amplify Ideas: Group Polarization and Groupthink

Groups have a sneaky way of intensifying our feelings or beliefs. Let's break this down:

Group Polarization: Imagine discussing a topic you feel strongly about with a group of like-minded people. By the end of the discussion, you might feel even more passionate about your stance. That's group polarization in action—groups can make our views more extreme.

Groupthink: Now, picture being in a team where everyone just nods along, without questioning or offering different perspectives. This uncritical conformity, where the desire for harmony trumps making the best decisions, is called groupthink. It's like being in an echo chamber where only one voice is heard, even if it's singing the wrong tune.

Obedience and Disobedience: Two Sides of the Same Coin

Following orders can sometimes lead to positive outcomes, like teamwork and coordinated efforts. But what happens when those orders are harmful or unjust?

Consequences of Obedience: History has shown that blindly following authority can lead to atrocities. When people stop questioning and just obey, they may find themselves doing things they'd never have thought possible.

Consequences of Disobedience: Standing up against unjust orders can be tough and might lead to backlash. However, acts of civil disobedience have also sparked positive social change throughout history.

So, as we navigate the world of conformity and group influence, it's vital to remember that these forces have their pros and cons. It's all about finding that balance, knowing when to go with the flow and when to paddle our own way. The next chapters will give you a toolkit to do just that, ensuring you're not just a leaf carried by the wind, but the wind itself.

Chapter 7: The Many Faces of Conformity

Conformity adapts like a shape shifter, blending into different environments and social spheres. Let's explore some of the key spaces where its influence takes hold.

Family and Peer Groups

Families sow the first seeds of norms into our fresh minds as children. The desire to please parents and fit in with friends makes conformity feel like a comforting blanket during youth.

School and Workplace

The halls of high school and office cubicles hum with an unspoken need to belong. These institutions reward following the herd, penalize sticking out. Is silence compliance or survival?

Political and Religious Groups

The lure of shared identity and purpose make conformity seductive in these spheres. To stay in the tribe, we echo their chants and don their armor. But at what cost to open minds?

Online Communities and Social Media

Virtual groups breed viral norms. Trends and ideas spread like wildfire, compelling us to conform if we crave likes and visibility. The tools may be new, but conformity's end-goal is ancient: to be part of the flock.

In every realm, conformity serves a purpose. Survival, connection, community - fundamental human needs. But in what contexts does conformity's cost to freedom become too great? Perhaps by shining light on its shapeshifting nature, we gain power over its hold.

Chapter 8: Through the Looking Glass: Stories of Conformity and Group Influence

Ever been engrossed in a movie scene where a character is torn between following the crowd and standing by their beliefs? Or a protagonist struggling to voice their opinion amidst a dominant group? Welcome to the real-life cinema of conformity and group influence! Let's immerse ourselves in some illustrative tales and unravel the mysteries behind the choices made.

The Office Outfit Dilemma

Scene: Jamie started a new job at a high-end advertising firm. On her first day, she noticed that most of her colleagues dressed in dark, formal colors. The next day, even though Jamie loved bright outfits, she opted for a muted black and grey ensemble.

Analysis: Jamie's choice to switch her dressing style is a classic example of normative influence, where she conformed to fit in and be accepted by her peers, even if it meant suppressing her own style.

A Voice Against the Popular Opinion

Scene: At a local town meeting, the majority supported building a mall in place of a small park. Max, however, valued the green space and its importance for the community. He was nervous, but he stood up and voiced his concerns.

Analysis: Max's decision to speak out against the popular vote shows the strength to resist groupthink. While the majority prioritized commercial development, Max prioritized community welfare, emphasizing the importance of individual voices in group settings.

The "Viral" Restaurant

Scene: A new restaurant opened in town. Influencers and locals raved about it on social media, creating a buzz. Sarah wasn't really keen on trying it, given her preference for home-cooked meals. But with all the hype, she felt she might be missing out. Eventually, she dined there.

Analysis: Sarah's choice was influenced by the informational influence—believing that the group must know something she doesn't. The widespread acclaim made her question her preferences and gave the restaurant a try.

The School Project Group Crisis

Scene: In a school project group of five, four members agreed on an idea without much discussion. Lisa, however, noticed some critical flaws. She hesitated initially but then pointed them out. The group, initially resistant, eventually recognized the problems and appreciated Lisa's input.

Analysis: The group's initial agreement is a nod to groupthink, where harmony is prioritized over critical evaluation. Lisa's intervention broke this cycle, highlighting the value of diverse perspectives and constructive criticism.

Conformity at the Charity Event

Scene: At a charity event, when a popular celebrity made a generous donation, many followed suit, even those who initially planned to contribute less.

Analysis: This is a classic scenario of normative influence. People conformed to the behavior set by a popular figure, influenced by the desire to be perceived in a positive light, akin to the celebrity.

By looking at these stories, we see reflections of ourselves, our choices, and the invisible strings of conformity and group influence that sometimes guide them. Recognizing these patterns is the first step. As we journey ahead, we'll equip ourselves with strategies to make choices that truly resonate with who we are, rather than just echoing the crowd.

Chapter 9: When Conformity Meets Its Match

Conformity may seem inevitable as gravity, but rebellion simmers in the human spirit. Let's explore when lone wolves turn the tide against the herd.

The Role of Minority Influence

Outnumbered non-conformists still plant seeds of change. By voicing original views consistently, a stubborn minority can gradually sway the majority. Resistance is not futile.

The Boomerang Effect

Push conformity too far and the oppressed push back. Forbidden acts become tempting. If conformity feels forceful, rebellious souls revolt. Suppression breeds discontent.

Acts of Non-Conformity and Civil Disobedience

Bold individuals have shattered norms through history. Rosa Parks refusing her seat, students protesting injustice - non-conformists speak truth to power.

Factors Influencing Resistance

While conformity allures those craving belonging, non-conformity blossoms in those valuing independence. Rebellion simmers in those denied freedom and respect. We resist when conformity conflicts with our core values.

Conformity and dissent form an eternal dance. The group sways us with belonging, but the rebel whispers freedom's call. Between compliance and resistance lies the struggle for truth. The dance continues...

Chapter 10: Navigating the Sea of Influence: Charting Your Own Course

Imagine sailing on a vast ocean, where the currents of conformity and group influence try to steer you off your chosen path. Wouldn't it be wonderful to have a compass and some navigational tools to keep you on track? Dive in as we equip ourselves to not just float with the tide, but to steer our ship confidently through the waves.

Turning on the Brain's Spotlight: Promoting Critical Thinking

Just like a detective examines every clue, we too can dissect the influences around us:

Ask Questions: Every time you feel swayed by the group, ask yourself - "Is this what I truly believe?" or "Why do I feel the need to go along?"

Research and Reflect: Before making decisions, especially major ones, take time to research and reflect on all aspects, rather than going with the popular choice.

Championing Voices of All Colors: Encouraging Diversity and Dissent

A painting is richer with many colors. Similarly, diverse voices make a group richer:

Open Platforms: Create spaces where everyone feels safe to voice their opinions, even if they're unpopular.

Celebrate Differences: Rather than viewing dissent as a challenge, see it as an opportunity for growth and learning.

Mirror, Mirror on the Wall: Cultivating Self-Awareness and Assertiveness

Knowing oneself is the first step to warding off unwanted influences:

Introspection: Regularly take a moment to understand your feelings, beliefs, and values. Journals or diaries can be a great way to reflect.

Speak Up: It might be challenging at first, but standing up for what you believe in is empowering. Start with small steps, like voicing your opinion in a group chat, and gradually build up your assertiveness.

The Captain's Role: Leadership in Preventing Negative Group Influence

A good leader isn't just someone who leads the charge but ensures every team member is walking their authentic path:

Lead by Example: Leaders can set the tone by showcasing transparency, openness, and respect for all opinions.

Foster Inclusivity: Encourage teams to have members from varied backgrounds and experiences. This naturally reduces the chances of groupthink.

Training and Workshops: Organize sessions on critical thinking, assertiveness, and the risks of conformity. When people are aware of these influences, they're better equipped to handle them.

As we wrap up this chapter, picture yourself with a strengthened ship, a reliable compass, and a clear map. With these tools in hand, you're ready to sail the vast ocean of life, making authentic choices, and charting a course that's truly yours. The waves of conformity and group influence might still come, but you'll be ready to navigate them like a seasoned sailor. Onward to new horizons!

The Final Curtain

Our journey exploring the social forces that sway us is coming to an end. Let's reflect on what we've learned before stepping back into the dance of life.

Recap of Key Points

We've uncovered conformity's shapeshifting nature, blending into groups and cultures. The longing to belong makes us susceptible, but self-awareness is the antidote. Though influence tugs at our strings, we can still dance to our own song.

The Future of Research

New technologies and social contexts offer insight into conformity's continuing grip - but also inspiration to transcend it. Expanding knowledge helps us wield group power for good, while nurturing freedom. There is hope on the horizon.

Personal and Societal Implications

Will we let groupsThink for us, or think freely for ourselves? The choice between belonging and autonomy is one we face again and again. This journey illuminates a path of integrity. Not conformity for its own sake, but rooted in connection and care for all people.

The curtain falls but the performance continues, moment by moment, choice by choice. We step back into the dance, a little wiser. The group's rhythm still pulses powerfully. But now we move to it in harmony with our own music - together, yet free.

About Freudian Trips

Welcome to Freudian Trips, your dedicated platform for diving deep into the world of psychology. We are more than just a YouTube channel or a book publisher. We are a beacon of enlightenment, making complex psychological concepts accessible and engaging for all.

Our YouTube channel is a rich repository of psychology made simple. We take the profound and often complex ideas from the world of psychology and break them down into digestible, easy-to-understand content. From the foundational theories of Freud to the cognitive insights of Piaget, we cover a broad spectrum of psychological schools and thoughts, making psychology accessible to everyone, regardless of their background or prior knowledge.

As a book publisher, we take the same approach, transforming intricate psychological theories into comprehensible narratives. Our books are not just collections of words, but vessels of wisdom that make psychology approachable and relatable. We believe that psychology should not be confined to academic circles, but should be available to all who seek to understand the human mind and behavior.

At Freudian Trips, we believe in the power of curiosity and the pursuit of knowledge. We are here to stoke the fires of your curiosity, to guide you on your intellectual journey, and to help you navigate the fascinating world of psychology.

If you are someone who is not afraid to question, to explore, and to learn, then you are in the right place. Join us on this journey of exploration, as we make psychology easy to understand, one concept at a time.

Be sure to visit our Youtube channel at: www.freudiantrips.com/youtube

You can also visit us on the web at www.freudiantrips.com

Welcome to The Freudian Trip community. Stay curious. Stay enlightened.